U.S. Department of Justice

Office of Justice Programs

Office of Juvenile Justice and Delinquency Prevention

Juvenile Offenders and Victims:

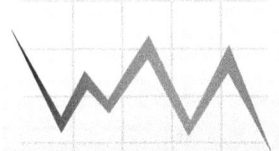

National Report Series

Bulletin

September 2011

This bulletin is part of the Juvenile Offenders and Victims National Report Series. The National Report *offers a comprehensive statistical overview of the problems of juvenile crime, violence, and victimization and the response of the juvenile justice system. During each interim year, the bulletins in the National Report Series provide access to the latest information on juvenile arrests, court cases, juveniles in custody, and other topics of interest. Each bulletin in the series highlights selected topics at the forefront of juvenile justice policymaking, giving readers focused access to statistics on some of the most critical issues. Together, the* National Report *and this series provide a baseline of facts for juvenile justice professionals, policymakers, the media, and concerned citizens.*

Trying Juveniles as Adults: An Analysis of State Transfer Laws and Reporting

Patrick Griffin, Sean Addie, Benjamin Adams, and Kathy Firestine

A Message From OJJDP

In the 1980s and 1990s, legislatures in nearly every state expanded transfer laws that allowed or required the prosecution of juveniles in adult criminal courts. The impact of these historic changes is difficult to assess inasmuch as there are no national data sets that track youth who have been tried and sentenced in the criminal justice system. Moreover, state data are hard to find and even more difficult to assess accurately.

In addition to providing the latest overview of state transfer laws and practices, this bulletin comprehensively examines available state-level data on juveniles adjudicated in the criminal justice system. In documenting state reporting practices regarding the criminal processing of youth and identifying critical information gaps, it represents an important step forward in understanding the impact of state transfer laws.

Currently, only 13 states publicly report the total number of their transfers, and even fewer report offense profiles, demographic characteristics, or details regarding processing and sentencing. Although nearly 14,000 transfers can be derived from available 2007 sources, data from 29 states are missing from that total.

To obtain the critical information that policymakers, planners, and other concerned citizens need to assess the impact of expanded transfer laws, we must extend our knowledge of the prosecution of juveniles in criminal courts. The information provided in these pages and the processes used to attain it will help inform the focus and design of additional federally sponsored research to that end.

Jeff Slowikowski
Acting Administrator

All states set boundaries where childhood ends and adult criminal responsibility begins

Transfer laws alter the usual jurisdictional age boundaries for exceptional cases

State juvenile courts with delinquency jurisdiction handle cases in which "juveniles" are accused of acts that would be crimes if "adults" committed them. Generally, these terms are defined solely by age. In most states, youth accused of violating the law before turning 18 years old come under the original jurisdiction of the juvenile courts, whereas those accused of violating the law on or after their 18th birthdays have their cases processed in criminal courts. Some states draw the juvenile/adult line at the 17th birthday, and a few draw it at the 16th birthday.

However, all states have transfer laws that allow or require criminal prosecution of some young offenders, even though they fall on the juvenile side of the jurisdictional age line.

Transfer laws are not new, but legislative changes in recent decades have greatly expanded their scope. As a result, the transfer "exception" has become a far more prominent feature of the nation's response to youthful offending.

Most states have multiple transfer mechanisms

Transfer laws vary considerably from state to state, particularly in terms of flexibility and breadth of coverage, but all fall into three basic categories:

- **Judicial waiver laws** allow juvenile courts to waive jurisdiction on a case-by-case basis, opening the way for criminal prosecution. A case that is subject to waiver is filed originally in juvenile court but may be transferred with a judge's approval, based on articulated standards, following a formal hearing. Even though all states set minimum thresholds and prescribe standards for waiver, the waiver decision is usually at the discretion of the judge. However, some states make waiver presumptive in certain classes of cases, and some even specify circumstances under which waiver is mandatory.

- **Prosecutorial discretion or concurrent jurisdiction laws** define a class of cases that may be brought in either juvenile or criminal court. No hearing is held to determine which court is appropriate, and there may be no formal standards for deciding between them. The decision is entrusted entirely to the prosecutor.

- **Statutory exclusion laws** grant criminal courts exclusive jurisdiction over certain classes of cases involving juvenile-age offenders. If a case falls within a statutory exclusion category, it must be filed originally in criminal court.

All states have at least one of the above kinds of transfer law. In addition, many have one or more of the following:

- **"Once adult/always adult" laws** are a special form of exclusion requiring criminal prosecution of any juvenile who has been criminally prosecuted in the past—usually without regard to the seriousness of the current offense.

- **Reverse waiver laws** allow juveniles whose cases are in criminal court to petition to have them transferred to juvenile court.

- **Blended sentencing laws** may either provide juvenile courts with criminal sentencing options (juvenile blended sentencing) or allow criminal courts to impose juvenile dispositions (criminal blended sentencing).

Nearly all states give courts discretion to waive jurisdiction over individual cases

A total of 45 states have laws designating some category of cases in which waiver of jurisdiction may be considered, generally on the prosecutor's motion, and granted on a discretionary basis. This is the oldest and still the most common form of transfer law, although most states have other, less traditional forms as well.

Discretionary waiver statutes prescribe broad standards to be applied, factors to be considered, and procedures to be followed in waiver decisionmaking and require that prosecutors bear the burden of proving that waiver is appropriate. Although waiver standards and evidentiary factors vary from state to state, most take into account both the nature of the alleged crime and the individual youth's age, maturity, history, and rehabilitative prospects.

In addition, most states set a minimum threshold for waiver eligibility: generally a minimum age and a specified type or level of offense, and sometimes a sufficiently serious record of previous delinquency. Waiver thresholds are often quite low, however. In a few states—such as Alaska, Kansas, and Washington—prosecutors may ask the court to waive virtually any juvenile delinquency case. As a practical matter, however, even in these states, waivers are likely to be relatively rare. Nationally, the proportion of juvenile cases in which prosecutors seek waiver is not known, but waiver is granted in less than 1% of petitioned delinquency cases.

Most states have multiple ways to impose adult sanctions on offenders of juvenile age

State	Judicial waiver			Prosecutorial discretion	Statutory exclusion	Reverse waiver	Once an adult always an adult	Blended sentencing	
	Discretionary	Presumptive	Mandatory					Juvenile	Criminal
Number of states	45	15	15	15	29	24	34	14	18
Alabama	■				■		■		
Alaska	■	■			■			■	
Arizona	■			■	■	■	■		
Arkansas	■			■		■		■	■
California	■	■		■		■	■		■
Colorado	■	■				■	■	■	■
Connecticut			■					■	
Delaware	■		■		■		■		
Dist. Of Columbia	■	■		■			■		
Florida	■			■	■		■		■
Georgia	■		■	■	■	■	■		
Hawaii	■						■		
Idaho	■				■				■
Illinois	■	■	■		■		■	■	■
Indiana	■		■		■		■		
Iowa	■				■	■	■		■
Kansas	■	■					■		
Kentucky	■		■		■	■			■
Louisiana	■		■	■	■				
Maine	■	■					■		
Maryland	■					■			
Massachusetts								■	■
Michigan	■			■			■	■	■
Minnesota	■	■					■	■	
Mississippi	■				■	■	■		
Missouri	■						■		■
Montana				■	■	■		■	
Nebraska				■		■			■
Nevada	■	■			■	■	■		
New Hampshire	■	■					■		
New Jersey	■	■	■						
New Mexico					■			■	■
New York					■	■			
North Carolina	■		■				■		
North Dakota	■	■	■				■		
Ohio	■		■				■	■	
Oklahoma	■			■	■	■	■		■
Oregon	■				■	■	■		
Pennsylvania	■	■			■	■	■		
Rhode Island	■	■	■				■	■	
South Carolina	■		■		■				
South Dakota	■				■	■	■		
Tennessee	■					■	■		
Texas	■						■	■	
Utah	■	■			■		■		
Vermont	■			■	■				■
Virginia	■		■	■	■	■			■
Washington	■				■		■		
West Virginia	■		■						■
Wisconsin	■				■	■	■		■
Wyoming	■			■		■			

Note: Table information is as of the end of the 2009 legislative session.

Most states allow juvenile court judges to waive jurisdiction over certain cases and transfer them to criminal court

State	Any criminal offense	Certain felonies	Capital crimes	Murder	Certain person offenses	Certain property offenses	Certain drug offenses	Certain weapon offenses
Alabama	14							
Alaska	NS							
Arizona		NS						
Arkansas		14	14	14	14			14
California	16							
Colorado		12			12	12		
Delaware	NS							
Dist. of Columbia	16	15						NS
Florida	14							
Georgia	15		13		13			
Hawaii		14		NS				
Idaho	14	NS		NS	NS	NS	NS	
Illinois	13							
Indiana		14		10			16	
Iowa	14							
Kansas	10							
Kentucky		14	14					
Louisiana				14	14			
Maine		NS						
Maryland	15			NS				
Michigan		14						
Minnesota		14						
Mississippi	13							
Missouri		12						
Nevada	14	14						
New Hampshire		15		13	13			
New Jersey	14			14	14	14	14	14
North Carolina		13						
North Dakota	16				14			
Ohio		14						
Oklahoma		NS						
Oregon		15		NS	NS	15		
Pennsylvania		14						
Rhode Island	NS	16	NS					
South Carolina	16	14			NS	NS		14	14
South Dakota		NS						
Tennessee	16				NS	NS		
Texas		14	14				14	
Utah		14						
Vermont				10	10	10		
Virginia		14						
Washington	NS							
West Virginia		NS		NS	NS	NS	NS	
Wisconsin	15	14		14	14	14	14	
Wyoming	13							

Notes: An entry in the column below an offense category means that there is at least one offense in that category for which a juvenile may be waived from juvenile court to criminal court. The number indicates the youngest possible age at which a juvenile accused of an offense in that category may be waived. "NS" means no age restriction is specified for an offense in that category. Table information is as of the end of the 2009 legislative session.

In presumptive waiver cases, the burden of proof shifts to the juvenile

In 15 states, presumptive waiver laws define a category of cases in which waiver from juvenile to criminal court is presumed appropriate. Statutes in these states leave the decision in the hands of a judge but weight it in favor of transfer. A juvenile who meets age, offense, or other statutory thresholds for presumptive waiver must present evidence rebutting the presumption, or the court will grant waiver and the case will be tried in criminal court.

State laws may require juvenile court judges to waive jurisdiction in certain cases

Fifteen states require juvenile courts to waive jurisdiction over cases that meet specified age/offense or prior record criteria. Cases subject to mandatory waiver are initiated in juvenile court, but the court has no other role than to confirm that the statutory requirements for mandatory waiver are met.

Functionally, a mandatory waiver law resembles a statutory exclusion, removing a designated category of cases from juvenile court jurisdiction. However, the juvenile court may retain power to make necessary orders relating to appointment of counsel, detention, and other preliminary matters.

Nonjudicial transfer cases bypass juvenile courts altogether

Only 15 states now rely solely on traditional hearing-based, judicially controlled forms of transfer: Connecticut, Hawaii, Kansas, Kentucky, Maine, Missouri, New Hampshire, New Jersey, North Carolina,

North Dakota, Ohio, Rhode Island, Tennessee, Texas, and West Virginia. In these states, all cases against juvenile-age offenders (except those who have already been criminally prosecuted once) begin in juvenile court and must be literally transferred, by individual court order, to courts with criminal jurisdiction.

In all other states, cases against some accused juveniles are filed directly in criminal court. Youth subject to direct criminal filing in these states may nevertheless be entitled to make an individualized case for juvenile handling at "reverse waiver" hearings before criminal court judges. Not all states allow this, however, and others do not allow it in some categories of cases.

Prosecutors' discretion to opt for criminal handling is often unfettered

Laws in 15 states designate some category of cases in which both juvenile and criminal courts have jurisdiction, so prosecutors may choose to file in either one court or the other. The choice is considered to be within the prosecutor's executive discretion, comparable with the charging decision.

In fact, prosecutorial discretion laws are usually silent regarding standards, protocols, or appropriate considerations for decisionmaking. Even in those few states where statutes provide some general guidance to prosecutors, or at least require them to develop their own decisionmaking guidelines, there is no hearing, no evidentiary record, and no opportunity for defendants to test (or even to know) the basis for a prosecutor's decision to proceed in criminal court. As a result, it is possible that prosecutorial discretion laws in some places operate like statutory exclusions, sweeping whole categories into criminal court with little or no individualized consideration.

Some states designate circumstances in which the burden of proof in a waiver hearing is shifted to the juvenile

State	Any criminal offense	Certain felonies	Capital crimes	Murder	Certain person offenses	Certain property offenses	Certain drug offenses	Certain weapon offenses
Alaska					NS			
California		14		14	14	14	14	
Colorado*		12		12	12			
Dist. Of Columbia†	15			15	15	15		
Illinois		15					15	
Kansas†	14	14			14		14	
Maine				NS	NS			
Minnesota		16						
Nevada†	14				14			
New Hampshire		15		15	15		15	
New Jersey		14		14	14	14	14	14
North Dakota		14		14	14		14	
Pennsylvania					14	14		
Rhode Island*	NS							
Utah		16		16	16	16		16

* In Colorado and Rhode Island, the presumption is applied against juveniles with certain kinds of histories.

† In the District of Columbia, Kansas, and Nevada, the presumption applies to any offense committed with a firearm.

Notes: An entry in the column below an offense category means that there is at least one offense in that category for which a juvenile is presumed to be an appropriate candidate for waiver to criminal court. The number indicates the youngest possible age at which a juvenile accused of an offense in that category is subject to the presumption. "NS" means no age restriction is attached to the presumption for an offense in that category. Table information is as of the end of the 2009 legislative session.

In some states, waiver is mandatory once the juvenile court judge determines that certain statutory criteria have been met

State	Certain felonies	Capital crimes	Murder	Certain person offenses	Certain property offenses	Certain drug offenses	Certain weapon offenses
Connecticut	14	14	14				
Delaware	15		NS	NS	16	16	
Georgia			14	14	15		
Illinois	15						
Indiana	NS					16	
Kentucky	14						
Louisiana			15	15			
New Jersey	16		16	16	16	16	16
North Carolina		13					
North Dakota			14	14		14	
Ohio	14		14	16	16		
Rhode Island			17	17			
South Carolina	14						
Virginia			14	14			
West Virginia	14		14	14	14		

Notes: An entry in the column below an offense category means that there is at least one offense in that category for which waiver to criminal court is mandatory. The number indicates the youngest possible age at which a juvenile accused of an offense in that category is subject to mandatory waiver. "NS" means no age restriction is specified for an offense in that category. Table information is as of the end of the 2009 legislative session.

Statutory exclusion laws restrict juvenile courts' delinquency jurisdiction

A total of 29 states have statutes that simply exclude some juvenile-age offenders from the jurisdiction of their juvenile courts, generally by defining the term "child" for delinquency purposes to leave out youth who meet certain age/offense or prior record criteria. Because such youth cannot by definition be "delinquent children," their cases are handled entirely in criminal court.

Many states make no distinction between minors and adults in enforcing traffic, boating, hunting, fishing and similar laws and ordinances—and may process all violations in criminal courts. Statutory exclusion laws are different, however, in that they make special exceptions for offending behavior that would otherwise be the responsibility of juvenile delinquency courts.

Murder is the offense most commonly singled out by statutory exclusion laws. In Massachusetts, Minnesota, and New Mexico, exclusion laws apply only to accused murderers. In all other states with exclusion statutes, murder is included along with other serious or violent felonies.

Some states exclude less serious offenses, especially where older juveniles or those with serious delinquency histories are involved. Montana law excludes 17-year-olds accused of a wide range of offenses, including attempted burglary, attempted arson, and attempted drug possession. Mississippi excludes all felonies that 17-year-olds commit as well as armed felonies that juveniles 13 or older commit. Utah excludes all felonies committed by 16-year-olds who have already been securely confined once, and Arizona excludes all felonies committed by those as young as 15, provided they have previously been disposed as juveniles more than once for felony-level offenses.

Some states allow prosecutors to file certain categories of cases in juvenile or criminal court

State	Any criminal offense	Certain felonies	Capital crimes	Murder	Certain person offenses	Certain property offenses	Certain drug offenses	Certain weapon offenses
Arizona		14						
Arkansas		16	14	14	14			
California		14	14	14	14	14	14	
Colorado		14		14	14	14		
Dist. of Columbia				16	16	16		
Florida	16	16	NS	14	14	14		14
Georgia			NS					
Louisiana				15	15	15	15	
Michigan		14		14	14	14	14	
Montana				12	12	16	16	16
Nebraska	16	NS						
Oklahoma		16		15	15	15	16	15
Vermont	16							
Virginia				14	14			
Wyoming	13	14		14	14	14		

Notes: An entry in the column below an offense category means that there is at least one offense in that category that is subject to criminal prosecution at the option of the prosecutor. The number indicates the youngest possible age at which a juvenile accused of an offense in that category is subject to criminal prosecution. "NS" means no age restriction is specified for an offense in that category. Table information is as of the end of the 2009 legislative session.

Many states exclude certain serious offenses from juvenile court jurisdiction

State	Any criminal offense	Certain felonies	Capital crimes	Murder	Certain person offenses	Certain property offenses	Certain drug offenses	Certain weapon offenses
Alabama		16	16				16	
Alaska					16	16		
Arizona		15		15	15			
California				14	14			
Delaware		15						
Florida				16	NS	16	16	
Georgia				13	13			
Idaho				14	14	14	14	
Illinois		15		13	15			15
Indiana		16		16	16		16	16
Iowa		16					16	16
Louisiana				15	15			
Maryland			14	16	16			16
Massachusetts				14				
Minnesota				16				
Mississippi		13	13					
Montana				17	17	17	17	17
Nevada	16*	NS		NS	16			
New Mexico				15				
New York				13	13	14		14
Oklahoma				13				
Oregon				15	15			
Pennsylvania				NS	15			
South Carolina		16						
South Dakota		16						
Utah		16		16				
Vermont				14	14	14		
Washington				16	16	16		
Wisconsin				10	10			

* In Nevada, the exclusion applies to any juvenile with a previous felony adjudication, regardless of the current offense charged, if the current offense involves the use or threatened use of a firearm.

Notes: An entry in the column below an offense category means that there is at least one offense in that category that is excluded from juvenile court jurisdiction. The number indicates the youngest possible age at which a juvenile accused of an offense in that category is subject to exclusion. "NS" means no age restriction is specified for an offense in that category. Table information is as of the end of the 2009 legislative session.

In most states, criminal prosecution renders a juvenile an "adult" forever

There is a special form of "automatic" transfer in 34 states for juveniles who have previously been prosecuted as adults. Most of these "once adult/always adult" laws are comprehensive, mandating criminal handling of all posttransfer offenses. However, Maryland, Michigan, Minnesota, and Texas have laws that apply only to posttransfer felonies, whereas Iowa, California, and Oregon require that the juveniles involved be at least 16.

Generally, once adult/always adult laws apply only to juveniles who were convicted of the offenses for which they were originally transferred. However, this is not necessary in all states, at least if the original transfer was based on an individualized judicial determination.

Many states give courts special flexibility in handling youth subject to transfer

Even states with automatic or prosecutor-controlled transfer laws often have compensating mechanisms that introduce some form of individualized judicial consideration into the process.

The most straightforward of these corrective mechanisms is the reverse waiver. A total of 24 states have reverse waiver laws, which allow juveniles whose cases are filed in criminal court to petition to have them removed to juvenile court, either for trial or disposition. Criminal court judges deciding reverse waiver motions usually consult the same kinds of standards and weigh the same factors as their juvenile court counterparts in discretionary waiver proceedings—but the burden of proof may be shifted to the juvenile as

the moving party. Moreover, even in states that have a reverse waiver option, it is not necessarily afforded to all transferred youth: 10 states with reverse waiver laws explicitly limit its availability.

Blended sentencing laws are also designed to provide a measure of individualization and flexibility in cases subject to transfer.

Laws in 18 states authorize their criminal courts, in sentencing juveniles who have been tried and convicted as adults, to impose juvenile dispositions rather than criminal ones under some circumstances. Such "criminal blended sentencing" statutes can function somewhat like reverse waiver laws, returning transferred juveniles on an individual basis to the juvenile correctional system for treatment and rehabilitation. However, they often require that a transferred juvenile receive a suspended criminal sentence, over and above any juvenile disposition. In any case, here again, criminal blended sentencing is commonly authorized only for a subset of those youth who are criminally convicted.

Juvenile blended sentencing laws in 14 states are sometimes seen as providing a "last chance" alternative for youth who would otherwise be transferred. A youth subject to the most common form of juvenile blended sentencing is tried in juvenile court and given a juvenile disposition —but in combination with a suspended criminal sentence. Although this may be preferable to straight criminal handling, the practical effects of juvenile blended sentencing statutes are not well understood. Because juvenile blended sentencing thresholds are actually lower than transfer thresholds in most states, there is a possibility that such laws, instead of providing a mitigating alternative to transfer, are instead being used for an "in-between" category of cases that would not otherwise have been transferred at all.

Some states give juvenile courts power to impose criminal sanctions in certain categories of cases

State	Any criminal offense	Certain felonies	Capital crimes	Murder	Certain person offenses	Certain property offenses	Certain drug offenses	Certain weapon offenses
Alaska					16			
Arkansas		14		NS	14			14
Colorado		NS			NS			
Connecticut		14			NS			
Illinois		13						
Kansas	10							
Massachusetts		14			14			14
Michigan		NS		NS	NS	NS	NS	
Minnesota		14						
Montana		12		NS	NS	NS	NS	NS
New Mexico		14		14	14	14		
Ohio		10		10				
Rhode Island		NS						
Texas		NS		NS	NS		NS	

Notes: An entry in the column below an offense category means that there is at least one offense in that category for which a juvenile may receive a blended sentence in juvenile court. The number indicates the youngest possible age at which a juvenile committing an offense in that category is subject to blended sentencing. "NS" indicates that, in at least one of the offense restrictions indicated, no minimum age is specified. Table information is as of the end of the 2009 legislative session.

State transfer laws changed radically in the closing decades of the 20th century

Before 1970, transfer in most states was court-ordered on a case-by-case basis

Laws allowing juvenile courts to waive jurisdiction over individual youth, sending "hard cases" to criminal courts for adult prosecution, could be found in some of the earliest juvenile codes and have always been relatively common. Most states had enacted such judicial waiver laws by the 1950s, and they had become nearly universal by the 1970s.

For the most part, these laws left transfer decisions to the discretion of juvenile court judges. Laws that made transfer "automatic" for certain categories—either by mandating waiver or by requiring that some charges be filed initially in criminal court—were rare and tended to apply only to rare offenses such as murder or capital crimes. Before 1970, only eight states had such laws.

Laws giving prosecutors the option to charge some juveniles in criminal court were even rarer. Only two states—Florida and Georgia—had prosecutorial discretion laws before 1970.

States adopted new transfer mechanisms in the 1970s and 1980s

During the next two decades, automatic and prosecutor-controlled forms of transfer proliferated steadily. In the 1970s alone, five states enacted new prosecutorial discretion laws, and seven more states adopted some form of automatic transfer.

By the mid-1980s, nearly all states had judicial waiver laws, 20 states had automatic transfer laws, and 7 states had prosecutorial discretion laws.

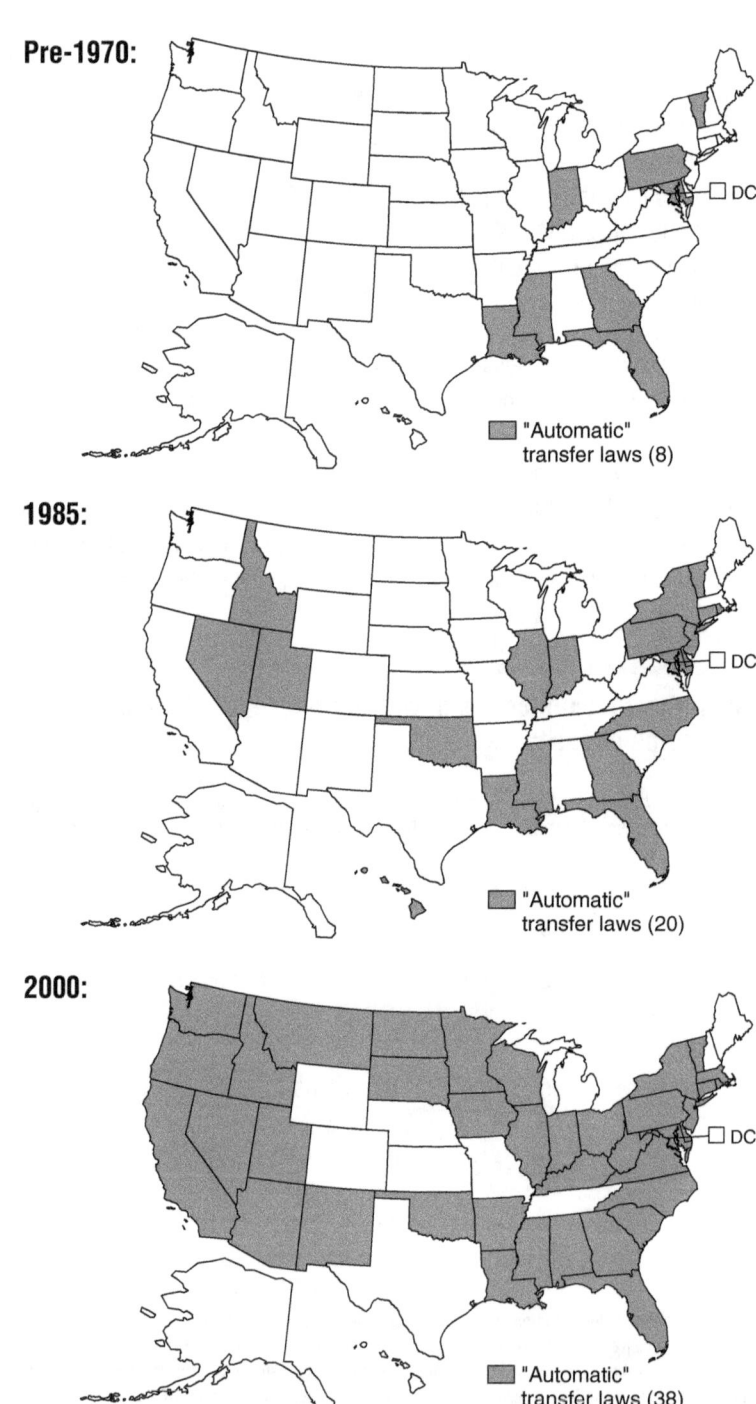

"Automatic" transfer laws proliferated in the decades after 1970 ...

Pre-1970:

☐ DC

■ "Automatic" transfer laws (8)

1985:

☐ DC

■ "Automatic" transfer laws (20)

2000:

☐ DC

■ "Automatic" transfer laws (38)

Sources: Pre-1970 and 1985 maps adapted from Feld's *The Juvenile Court Meets the Principle of the Offense: Legislative Changes to Juvenile Waiver Statutes* and Hutzler's *Juveniles as Criminals: 1980 Statutes Analysis*.

... as did prosecutorial discretion laws

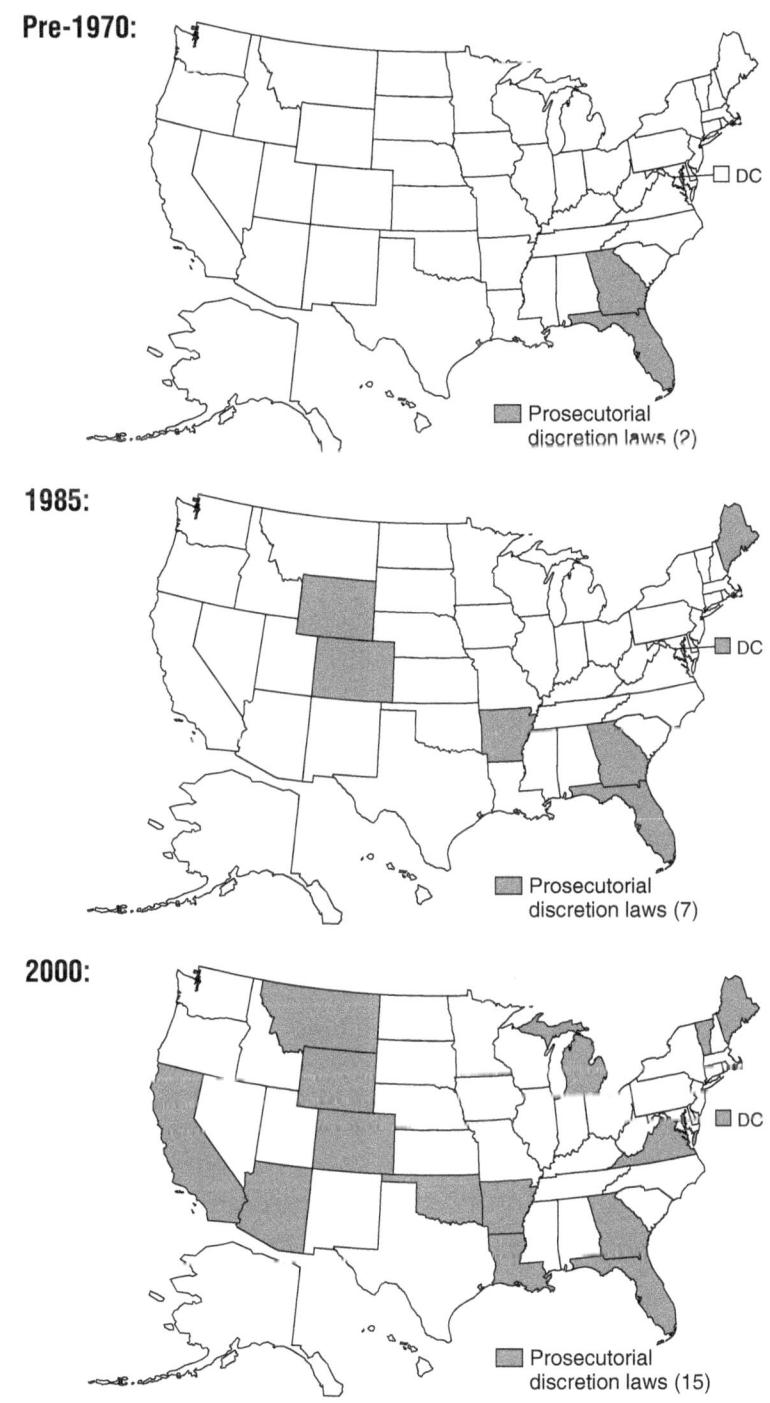

Pre-1970:

☐ DC

■ Prosecutorial discretion laws (?)

1985:

■ DC

■ Prosecutorial discretion laws (7)

2000:

■ DC

■ Prosecutorial discretion laws (15)

Sources: Pre-1970 and 1985 maps adapted from Feld's *The Juvenile Court Meets the Principle of the Offense: Legislative Changes to Juvenile Waiver Statutes* and Hutzler's *Juveniles as Criminals: 1980 Statutes Analysis.*

The surge in youth violence that peaked in 1994 helped shape current transfer laws

State transfer laws in their current form are largely the product of a period of intense legislative activity that began in the latter half of the 1980s and continued through the end of the 1990s. Prompted in part by public concern and media focus on the rise in violent youth crime that began in 1987 and peaked in 1994, legislatures in nearly every state revised or rewrote their laws to lower thresholds and broaden eligibility for transfer, shift transfer decisionmaking authority from judges to prosecutors, and replace individualized discretion with automatic and categorical mechanisms.

Between 1986 and the end of the 1990s, the number of states with automatic transfer laws jumped from 20 to 38, and the number with prosecutorial discretion laws rose from 7 to 15. Moreover, many states that had automatic or prosecutor-controlled transfer statutes expanded their coverage in such a way as to change their essential character. In Pennsylvania, for example, an exclusion law had been on the books since 1933—but had applied only to cases of murder. Amendments that took effect in 1996 transformed what had been a narrow and rarely used safety valve into a broad exclusion covering a long list of violent offenses.

In recent years, transfer laws have changed little

Transfer law changes since 2000 have been minor by comparison. No major new expansion has occurred. On the other hand, states have shown little tendency to reverse or even reconsider the expanded transfer laws already in place. Despite the steady decline in juvenile crime and violence rates since 1994, there has as yet been no discernible pendulum swing away from transfer.

For every 1,000 petitioned delinquency cases, about 9 are judicially waived to criminal court

Juvenile court data provide a detailed picture of waiver in the U.S.

Each year juvenile courts provide detailed delinquency case processing data to the National Juvenile Court Data Archive that the National Center for Juvenile Justice maintains. Using this information, NCJJ generates annual estimates of the number and characteristics of cases that juvenile court judges waive to criminal court in the nation as a whole. In 2007, using data contributed by more than 2,200 juvenile courts with jurisdiction over 81% of the nation's juvenile population, juvenile courts are estimated to have waived jurisdiction in about 8,500 cases—less than 1% of the total petitioned delinquency caseload.

Nearly half of all cases judicially waived to criminal court in 2007 involved a person offense as the most serious charge. Youth whose cases were waived were overwhelmingly males and tended to be older teens. Although a substantial proportion (37%) of waivers involved black youth, racial disparity in the use of judicial waiver has diminished. In 1994, juvenile courts waived cases involving black youth at 1.5 times the rate at which cases involving white youth were waived. By 2007, the disparity was reduced to 1.1 times the white rate.

The use of judicial waiver has declined steeply since 1994

The number of judicially waived cases hit a historic peak in 1994—when about 13,100 cases were waived—and has fallen 35% since that year. There are two sets of causes that might account for this trend:

The likelihood of judicial waiver among petitioned delinquency cases was lower in 2007 than in 1994 for all offense categories and demographic groups

Offense/demographic	Profile of judicially waived delinquency cases		Percentage of petitioned cases judicially waived to criminal court	
	1994	2007	1994	2007
Total cases waived	13,100	8,500	13,100	8,500
Most serious offense	100%	100%		
Person	42	48	2.6%	1.7%
Property	37	27	1.1	0.7
Drugs	12	13	2.1	1.0
Public order	9	11	0.6	0.3
Gender	100%	100%		
Male	95	90	1.7	1.1
Female	5	10	0.4	0.4
Age at referral	100%	100%		
15 or younger	13	12	0.3	0.2
16 or older	87	88	3.0	1.7
Race/ethnicity	100%	100%		
White	53	59	1.2	0.9
Black	44	37	1.8	1.0

Note: These data on cases judicially waived from juvenile court to criminal court do not include cases filed directly in criminal court via other transfer mechanisms.

Source: Authors' analysis of Puzzanchera et al.'s *Juvenile Court Statistics 2007*.

■ **Decreases in juvenile violent crime reduced the need for waiver.** Juvenile arrests for most crimes, and particularly for Violent Index offenses, have fallen almost every year since 1994. Because judicial waiver has historically served as a mechanism for removing serious and violent offenders from a juvenile system that was seen as ill-equipped to accommodate them, a reduction in serious and violent crime should naturally result in some reduction in the volume of waivers.

■ **New transfer mechanisms displaced waiver.** The nationwide proliferation and expansion of nontraditional transfer mechanisms also may have contributed to the reduction in waivers. In states with prosecutorial discretion or statutory exclusion laws, cases involving juvenile-age offenders can originate in criminal courts, bypassing the juvenile courts altogether. During the 1990s, law revisions in most states exposed more youth to these forms of transfer. Because these new laws were generally operating already by the mid-1990s, many juveniles who would previously have been candidates for waiver were subject to nonwaiver transfer instead. Overall transfer volume after 1994 could have stayed the same—or even continued to rise—even as waiver volume declined.

It is probable that both of these causes were at work and that declining waiver numbers reflect both overall juvenile crime trends and the diminished importance of judicial waiver relative to other transfer mechanisms.

Juvenile arrest and judicial waiver trends for serious violent offenses had similar patterns over the past two decades

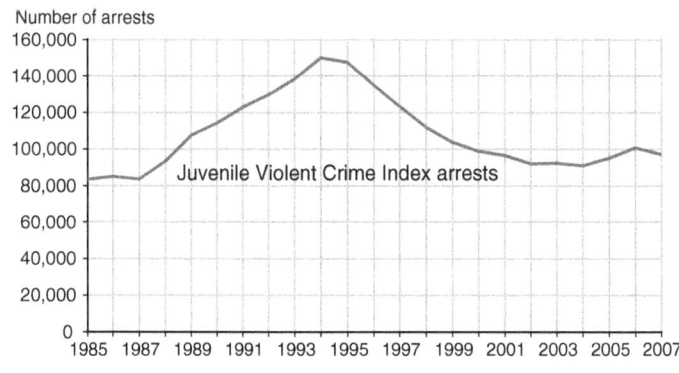

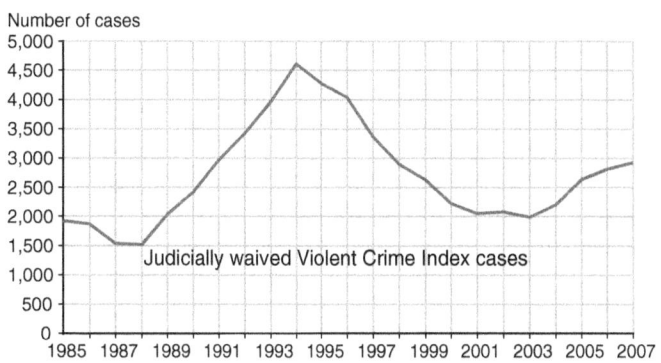

* The Violent Crime Index includes the offenses of murder and nonnegligent manslaughter, forcible rape, robbery, and aggravated assault.

■ From the mid-1980s to the peak in 1994, the number of juvenile arrests for Violent Crime Index offenses nearly doubled and then declined substantially through 2004 (down 39%). This decade-long decline was followed by an 11% increase over the next 2 years, and then a 4% decline between 2006 and 2007.

■ Similarly, the number of cases judicially waived for Violent Crime Index offenses tripled between 1988 and 1994 and then declined 57% through 2003. Between 2003 and 2007, the number of cases waived increased 47%.

Sources: Authors' analyses of FBI unpublished reports for 1980 through 1997, the FBI's *Crime in the United States* reports for 1998 through 2007, and Sickmund et al.'s *Easy Access to Juvenile Court Statistics 2007.*

National information on juvenile cases filed directly in criminal court is fragmentary

No national data set tracks cases that bypass juvenile courts

No data source exists that is comparable to the National Juvenile Court Data Archive for nonwaiver cases—those in which juveniles are processed in criminal court as a result of statutory exclusions or prosecutors' discretionary choices. Because they are filed in criminal court like other cases, involve defendants who are "adults" at least for criminal handling purposes, and represent an insignificant proportion of the criminal justice system's overall caseload, juvenile cases originating in criminal court can be very difficult to isolate statistically. Legal, definitional, and reporting variations from state to state also make it hard to aggregate what information is available. Although several federally sponsored criminal processing data collection efforts have shed some light on cases involving juvenile-age offenders, to date none has been designed to yield reliable national estimates of the overall volume and characteristics of these cases. As a result, at the national level, a big part of the picture of transfer is missing.

BJS research provides glimpses of transfer case characteristics

Available national statistics on criminal processing of juveniles come primarily from a handful of large-scale data gathering efforts that the federal Bureau of Justice Statistics (BJS) sponsors. Both the State Court Processing Statistics (SCPS) program and the National Judicial Reporting Program (NJRP) periodically collect detailed information on felony cases in state criminal courts. Special analyses of data from both programs have yielded information on the relatively small subset of

felony cases that involve youth. The BJS-sponsored National Survey of Prosecutors (NSP) has likewise been used to collect basic information on criminal prosecution of juveniles in the states.

The SCPS collects demographic, offense, processing, and sentencing information on felony defendants from a sample of 40 large urban jurisdictions that are representative of the nation's 75 largest counties. For the 1998 SCPS, BJS used an oversampling technique to capture sufficient information on criminally processed juveniles to support a special analysis of this subgroup. Although it did not produce a sample that was representative of the nation as a whole—and so cannot tell us about juveniles charged in criminal court with misdemeanors rather than felonies, or those processed outside the nation's 75 largest counties—the study did provide useful insight into urban transfer cases in which serious offenses are alleged:

- **Volume.** About 7,100 juveniles were criminally processed for felonies in the 40 sampled counties during 1998.

- **Transfer mechanism.** Less than a quarter of the cases reached criminal court via judicial waiver. More common were exclusion cases (42%) and prosecutorial direct files (35%).

- **Charges.** The most serious charge at arrest in about half of the cases was either robbery (31%) or assault (21%). The next most common charges were drug trafficking (11%) and burglary (8%).

- **Demographics.** Defendants were overwhelmingly male (96%) and predominantly black (62%).

The NJRP collects information on felony sentences in state courts. The 1996 NJRP

collected data from 344 counties, generating a subsample of juvenile-age felony cases that, while not statistically representative of all transferred juveniles, was large enough to enable researchers to explore ways in which juvenile cases differed from those of other convicted felons.

Compared with adult felons, the special analysis found, transferred juveniles were more likely than their adult counterparts to be male (96% versus 84%) and black (55% versus 45%). Juveniles were more likely than adults to have a person offense as their most serious offense at conviction (53% versus 17%) and far less likely to have a drug offense (11% versus 37%).

The majority of juvenile felony defendants in the 75 largest counties reached criminal court through nonjudicial transfer

Demographic	Percentage of juvenile felony defendants
Volume	7,100
Transfer mechanism	100.0%
Judicial waiver	23.7
Prosecutor direct file	34.7
Statutory exclusion	41.6
Most serious charge	100.0%
Violent offense	63.5
Property offense	17.7
Drug offense	15.1
Public order offense	3.5
Gender	100.0%
Male	95.8
Female	4.2
Race	100.0%
White	19.9
Black	62.2
Other	1.8
Hispanic	16.2

Source: Authors' adaptation of Rainville and Smith's *Juvenile Felony Defendants in Criminal Courts: Survey of 40 Counties, 1998.*

Most prosecutors' offices report trying juveniles as adults

The NSP is a regular BJS-sponsored survey of chief prosecutors who try felony cases in state courts of general jurisdiction. Its primary purpose is to collect basic information on office staffing, funding, caseloads, etc., but several recent surveys have asked respondents whether their offices proceeded against juveniles in criminal court and, if so, how many such cases were prosecuted in the 12 months preceding the survey. The 2005 NSP, which was a survey of a nationally representative sample of 310 prosecutors, found that about two-thirds of prosecutors' offices tried juveniles in criminal court. On the basis of the 2005 responses, it was estimated that about 23,000 juvenile cases had been criminally prosecuted nationwide during the 12 months preceding the survey.

Although the NSP information is useful as a starting point in assessing the criminal processing of youth, it must be handled with a certain amount of caution. Respondents were asked to give either the actual number of criminally prosecuted juvenile cases over the preceding 12-month period or their best estimates, but there is no way of knowing the basis for any estimates provided. In any case, the information elicited gives only an aggregate case total and does not contribute to understanding the characteristics or processing of those cases.

Transferred juvenile felons were far more likely than adult felons to be convicted of violent offenses

Demographic	Transferred juvenile felons	Adult felons
Most serious felony charge	100%	100%
Violent offense	53	17
Property offense	27	30
Drug offense	11	37
Weapons offense	3	3
Other offense	6	14
Gender	100%	100%
Male	96	84
Female	4	16
Race	100%	100%
White	43	53%
Black	55	45
Other	2	2

Source: Authors' adaptation of Levin, Langan, and Brown's *State Court Sentencing of Convicted Felons, 1996.*

A new BJS survey will help fill information gaps on criminal processing of juveniles nationally

BJS recently awarded a new national survey effort to Westat and subcontractor, the National Center for Juvenile Justice, with the goal of generating accurate and reliable case processing statistics for juveniles charged as adults. The Survey of Juveniles Charged as Adults in Criminal Courts will be the first effort of its kind that focuses solely on generating national data on youth in criminal court; it is likely to contribute substantially to the knowledge regarding the criminal processing of youth. Drawing from a sample of felony and misdemeanor cases filed against youth in criminal courts who were younger than 18—including both transfer cases and cases involving youth who are considered adults under their states' jurisdictional age laws—the survey will gather information on offender demographics and offense histories, arrest and arraignment charges, transfer mechanisms, and case processing and disposition.

Most states do not track and account for all of their juvenile transfer cases

The Transfer Data Project documented state transfer reporting practices

In the absence of any one data source that would make it possible to arrive at an accurate estimate of the number of juvenile-age offenders prosecuted in criminal courts nationwide, it is necessary to look instead to a variety of state sources. Unfortunately, information from these scattered sources is fragmentary, hard to find, and harder to analyze.

In an effort to document reliable sources of state-level data on juvenile transfers, identify crucial gaps in available information on transferred youth and, if possible, fill in the national data picture on transfer, NCJJ conducted a Transfer Data Project in 2009. The project, a component of the OJJDP-funded National Juvenile Justice Data Analysis Project, began with a structured search for any published or online reports that official sources regularly issued within the 1995–2009 time frame and containing any state-level statistics on criminal prosecution of juveniles. Following this initial search, project staff conducted a snowball survey of likely data keepers in individual states, including contributors to the National Juvenile Court Data Archive, asking for further information, clarification, and leads. In all, 63 officials were contacted via e-mail and telephone followups, including representatives of state juvenile justice agencies, state judicial administrative offices, state prosecutors' agencies, and state statistical analysis centers. Most state respondents referred NCJJ staff to published reports containing pertinent statistics, redirected queries to other state officials, or confirmed that the information sought was not collected at the state level. However, officials in nine states were able to supply NCJJ directly with transfer numbers that resided in state information systems or had otherwise been collected at the state level but were not made available in public reports.

These data were analyzed along with state-published statistics on transfer, yielding the most complete picture currently available of juvenile transfer and transfer-reporting practice in the states. In addition to being summarized in this report, project findings regarding state transfer and reporting practice will be incorporated into the online summary of state transfer laws found on OJJDP's Statistical Briefing Book Web site, http://ojjdp.gov/ojstatbb/structure_process/faqs.asp.

Only 13 states publicly report all transfers

From the information that the Transfer Data Project assembled, it appears that only a small minority of states currently track and report comprehensive information regarding criminal prosecutions of juveniles. Indeed, only 13 states were identified as publicly reporting even the total number of their transfers, including cases of juveniles who reach criminal courts as a result of statutory exclusions or prosecutors' discretionary choices as well as judicial waiver decisions. States that publish information on the offense profiles or demo-graphic characteristics of these youth, or provide details regarding their processing or sentencing, are even rarer.

With respect to their reporting of the *number* of transfers only, states fall into four categories:

■ **Publicly report all transfers (13 states).** A few of these states report only a bare annual total—the number of criminally prosecuted youth, the number of criminal cases involving youth, or both—but most report something more, such as age, race, or gender information on transferred youth, how they reached criminal court, what their offenses were, or how their cases were resolved.

■ **Publicly report some but not all transfers (10 states).** Commonly, these states report the number of cases that are sent to criminal court, following waiver proceedings in juvenile court, but not the number that are filed directly in criminal court.

■ **Contribute data to the National Juvenile Court Data Archive but do not otherwise report transfers (14 states).** States that contribute annual juvenile case processing data to the Archive that NCJJ maintains are, in effect, reporting information on judicially waived cases, although not to the public. NCJJ uses these data to prepare national waiver estimates but does not publish individual state waiver totals. Accordingly, Archive reporting does not help the field and members of the public understand how individual states' waiver laws are operating in practice.

■ **Do not report transfers at all (14 states).** These states do not contribute data on waived cases to the Archive, and NCJJ was unable to locate any other official reports containing their waiver and/or transfer totals. However, officials in five of these states responded to NCJJ's information requests by sharing recent data on transfer cases—which suggests that they already collect the pertinent information at the state level or, at least, are capable of collecting it.

About half of the states publicly report at least some information regarding criminal prosecutions of juveniles

State	Publicly report all transfers	Publicly report some but not all transfers	Contribute to the National Juvenile Court Data Archive but do not otherwise report transfers	Do not report transfers at all
Number of states	13	10	14	14
Alabama			■	
Alaska			■	
Arizona	■			
Arkansas				■
California	■			
Colorado				■
Connecticut			■	
Delaware				■
District of Columbia			■	
Florida	■			
Georgia			■	
Hawaii			■	
Idaho				■
Illinois		■		
Indiana				■
Iowa		■		
Kansas	■			
Kentucky				■
Louisiana		■		
Maine				■
Maryland		■		
Massachusetts				■
Michigan	■			
Minnesota		■		
Mississippi		■		
Missouri	■			
Montana	■			
Nebraska				■
Nevada			■	
New Hampshire				■
New Jersey			■	
New Mexico		■		
New York			■	
North Carolina	■			
North Dakota				■
Ohio	■			
Oklahoma		■		
Oregon	■			
Pennsylvania		■		
Rhode Island			■	
South Carolina		■		
South Dakota				■
Tennessee	■			
Texas	■			
Utah			■	
Vermont				■
Virginia			■	
Washington	■			
West Virginia			■	
Wisconsin			■	
Wyoming				■

Note: Table information is as of 2009.

States are more likely to track judicial waiver cases than other kinds of transfers

Relatively speaking, states do a better job of tracking cases that originate in juvenile court and are transferred to criminal court on an individualized basis. Transfer cases that bypass juvenile courts altogether are more commonly "lost" in states' general criminal processing statistics:

■ Of the 46 states that have judicial waiver laws, 20 publicly report annual waiver totals and 13 more report waivers to the National Juvenile Court Data Archive.

■ By contrast, of the 29 states with statutory exclusion laws requiring criminal prosecution of some juveniles, only 2 publicly report the total number of excluded cases, and 5 others report a combined total of all criminally prosecuted cases, without specifying the transfer mechanism employed.

■ Of the 15 states that have prosecutorial discretion laws, only 1 publicly reports the total number of cases filed in criminal court at prosecutors' discretion, and 4 others report an undifferentiated total of all criminally prosecuted cases.

The scarcity of information on cases involving youth prosecuted under exclusion and prosecutorial discretion laws presents a serious problem for those wishing to assess the workings, effectiveness, and overall impact of these laws. Even the few states that provide a count of excluded or direct-filed cases seldom report the kind of demographic, offense, sentencing, and other detail that is needed to inform judgments about whether laws entrusting transfer decisions to prosecutors rather than judges are being applied fairly and consistently. It is not clear whether these laws are targeting the most serious offenders and resulting in the kinds of sanctions lawmakers intended. And if these laws are operating as intended in one state, are they doing so in all the states that rely on such provisions?

The absence of information on cases transferred at prosecutors' discretion is particularly troubling. Some prosecutorial discretion laws are very broadly written. For example, in Nebraska and Vermont—neither of which currently publish annual transfer statistics—any youth who is at least 16 may be prosecuted as an adult at the prosecutor's option, regardless of the offense alleged. However, even states that limit prosecutors' discretionary authority to cases involving serious offenses do not thereby eliminate the possibility of unfair or inappropriate use of the authority.

Because statutory exclusion laws apply automatically to all juveniles who come within their provisions, they present less danger of inconsistent, unfair, or inappropriate enforcement. However, even apparently neutral laws may, in practice, fall more heavily on certain groups. Again, many exclusion laws apply to very broadly defined categories—all felony-grade offenses, for example, or all offenses in high-volume categories like assaults, robberies, burglaries, and drug offenses—that may, in practice, cover a variety of actual crime scenarios, from the very serious to the relatively trivial. Whether or not exclusion laws are working as intended—increasing the likelihood of prosecution, conviction, incarceration, and long sentences, and serving as a deterrent—is a question of fact that cannot be answered without more information than is generally available at present. Additional data are also needed to determine whether exclusion laws (1) impact certain groups more than others, (2) impact large numbers of youth whose offense profiles may be less serious than those originally envisioned, or (3) work differently from one state to another.

Few states publicly report data on cases transferred by statutory exclusion or prosecutorial discretion

State	Has judicial waiver	Reports judicial waiver to public	Reports judicial waiver to Archive	Has prose-cutorial discretion	Reports statutory discretion to public	Has statutory exclusion	Reports statutory exclusion to public
Number of states	46	20	28	15	5	29	7
Alabama	■		■			■	
Alaska	■		■			■	
Arizona	■	■	■	■	✳	■	✳
Arkansas	■			■			
California	■	■	■	■	✳	■	✳
Colorado	■			■			
Connecticut	■		■				
Delaware	■					■	
District of Columbia	■		■	■			
Florida	■	■	■	■	✳	■	✳
Georgia	■		■	■		■	
Hawaii	■		■				
Idaho	■					■	
Illinois	■	●				■	●
Indiana	■					■	
Iowa	■	■				■	
Kansas	■	■					
Kentucky	■						
Louisiana	■			■		■	
Maine	■						
Maryland	■	■	■			■	
Massachusetts						■	
Michigan	■	■	■		■		
Minnesota	■	■				■	
Mississippi	■	■				■	
Missouri	■	■					
Montana				■	✳	■	✳
Nebraska				■			
Nevada	■		■			■	
New Hampshire	■						
New Jersey	■		■				
New Mexico						■	
New York						■	
North Carolina	■		■				
North Dakota	■						
Ohio	■	■	■				
Oklahoma	■	■	■	■		■	
Oregon	■	✳	■			■	✳
Pennsylvania	■		■			■	
Rhode Island	■		■			■	
South Carolina	■	■	■			■	
South Dakota	■					■	
Tennessee	■	■	■				
Texas	■	■	■				
Utah	■					■	
Vermont	■			■		■	
Virginia	■			■			
Washington	■	■	■			■	■
West Virginia	■	■	■				
Wisconsin	■		■			■	
Wyoming	■			■			

● Partial reporting (not all jurisdictions).

✳ Combined total of transfer mechanisms (not separated out).

Note: Table information is as of 2009.

There are wide variations in the ways states document juvenile transfers

Only a few states report significant details about transfer cases

The Transfer Data Project's search for official state data on youth prosecuted as adults uncovered a broad range of approaches to reporting on transfers, particularly in terms of the completeness and level of detail of the information reported.

Arizona, California, and Florida can be regarded as exemplary states when it comes to collecting and regularly reporting detailed statistics on juveniles tried as adults. Although they do not report exactly the same things in the same ways, they do provide the field and the public with most of the basic information needed to assess the workings and impact of their juvenile transfer laws. Most other states—even among those that regularly track and report their annual juvenile transfer totals—report far fewer details regarding those cases.

Although there is no one "right" way to report information on juvenile transfer cases, reasonably complete documentation could be expected to cover each of the following general categories:

- **Total volume.** As noted previously, only 13 states report the total number of cases in which juvenile-age offenders are prosecuted in criminal court, the total number of juveniles prosecuted, or both.

- **Pathways.** Of these 13 states, 5 provide information showing how transfer cases reached the criminal system—whether by way of judicial waiver, prosecutors' discretionary decisions, or as a result of statutory exclusions. In six others, judicial waiver was the only transfer mechanism available.

- **Demographics.** Eight of the 13 states provide age, race/ethnicity, gender, or other demographic information on criminally prosecuted youth.

- **Offenses.** Only three of these states provide information on the offenses for which youth were transferred.

- **Processing outcomes.** Only one of these states—California—reports information on criminal court handling and disposition of transfer cases.

Available data show dramatic differences in states' transfer rates

Although the national picture is far from complete, rough comparisons among the subset of states that do track total transfers make it clear that there are striking variations in individual states' propensity to try juveniles as adults, even when differences in juvenile population sizes are taken into account.

Some state-to-state differences in per capita transfer rates are undoubtedly linked to differences in jurisdictional age boundaries. The lowest transfer rates among the 13 full-reporting states tend to be found in the states that set lower age boundaries for criminal court jurisdiction (Michigan, Missouri, North Carolina, and Texas). In these states, 17-year-olds (or in the case of North Carolina, 16- and 17-year-olds) must be taken out of the mix: They cannot be "transferred" for criminal prosecution because they are already within the original jurisdiction of the criminal courts. That leaves a transfer-eligible population that is younger and statistically less likely to be involved in serious offending. (Of course, if one were simply measuring the extent to which states criminally prosecute youth who are younger than 18, these states' rates would be among the highest.)

Differences in state transfer rates may also be explained, in part, by broad differences in the way transfer mechanisms

Offense and processing information on transfers is rarely reported

State	Total volume	Pathways	Demographics	Offenses	Processing outcomes
Number of states	13	11	8	3	1
Arizona	■	■	■	■	
California	■	■	■	■	■
Florida	■	■	■	■	
Kansas	■	*			
Michigan	■	■			
Missouri	■	*	■		
Montana	■		■		
North Carolina	■	*			
Ohio	■	*	■		
Oregon	■		■		
Tennessee	■	*	■		
Texas	■	*			
Washington	■	■			

* Waiver-only states.

Note: Table information is as of 2009.

work. In the six reporting states (Kansas, Missouri, North Carolina, Ohio, Tennessee, and Texas) that have only judicial waiver laws—even including those in which some waivers are mandated—average transfer rates are generally lower than those in the remaining seven states, which have statutory exclusion laws, prosecutorial discretion laws, or both.

However, it can be difficult to account for state transfer rate variations on the basis of legal structures alone. For instance, Tennessee appears to transfer juveniles far more often than Kansas (although both are waiver-only states) and, if anything, Tennessee law imposes more restrictions on the juvenile court's power to waive jurisdiction.

Average annual transfer rate,* 2003–2008:

Florida	164.7
Oregon	95.6
Arizona	83.7
Tennessee	42.6
Montana	41.6
Kansas	25.3
Washington	21.2
Missouri	20.9
California	20.6
Ohio	20.4
Michigan	12.4
Texas	8.6
North Carolina	7.1

*Cases per 100,000 juveniles ages 10 to upper age of juvenile court jurisdiction.

Notes: Table is intended for rough comparison only. Unit of count varies from state to state. Some states report by fiscal year, some by calendar year. Transfer volume was unavailable for Montana in 2005, 2006, and 2008 and for Washington in 2008.

Detailed transfer reporting in some states makes indepth comparison possible

Because they document their juvenile transfers more thoroughly than other states, data from Arizona, California, and Florida provide a considerably more nuanced picture of transfer in practice. Even though all three are populous "sunbelt"

states with large urban centers, significant crime, and a broadly similar array of transfer laws, official reports from the three states make clear that they have markedly different approaches to transfer.

Overall rates. The three states differ dramatically in their per capita transfer rates—with Florida being the clear outlier. Over the period from 2003 through 2008, Florida transferred youth at about twice the rate of Arizona and about eight times the rate of California. (In fact, Florida's rate was about five times the average transfer rate in the other 12 states that publicly reported total transfers during this period.) One part of the explanation is undoubtedly Florida's expansive prosecutorial discretion law, which permits prosecutors to opt for criminal handling of, among others, all 16- and 17-year-olds accused of felonies. (Only Nebraska and Vermont give prosecutors more

discretionary authority.) However, both Arizona and California prosecutors also have broad prosecutorial discretion provisions, suggesting that aggressive use of prosecutorial discretion in Florida may be a factor as well.

Transfer pathways. Although Florida has an extremely broad and flexible judicial waiver provision—authorizing waiver for any offense, providing the juvenile was at least 14 at the time of commission—judicial waiver is a relatively insignificant transfer mechanism there, accounting for only about 4% of total transfers from 2003 to 2008. In Arizona, 14% of transfers came by way of waiver, but waivers steadily declined over that period, both in absolute terms and as a proportion of total transfers.

In California, by contrast, about 40% of transfers from 2003 to 2008 were

California reports detailed case-processing outcomes for transferred youth

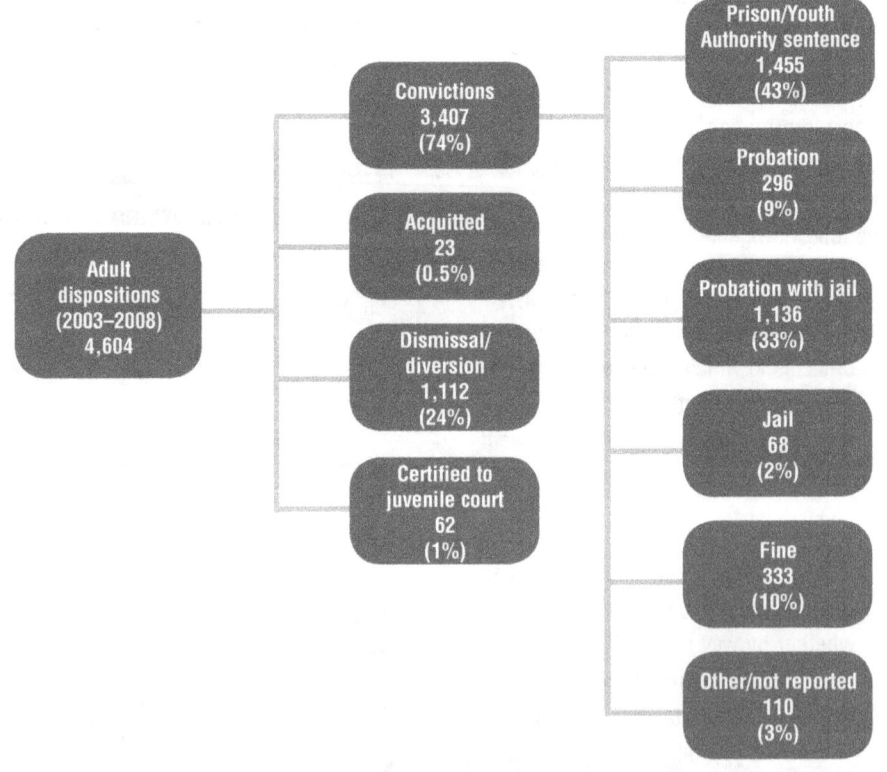

Source: Authors' analyses of California Office of the Attorney General reports available online.

waivers. California prosecutors may make a motion for "fitness hearings" for any 16- or 17-year-old, regardless of the offense alleged, and for younger offenders accused of more serious offenses. Moreover, where youth are accused of serious offenses or have serious prior records, they may be presumed to be unfit for juvenile court handling and must affirmatively prove otherwise. Perhaps because this shifting of the burden of proof makes the fitness hearing route easier for prosecutors, it is frequently used and is frequently successful: 71% of all fitness hearings from 2003 to 2008 resulted in remand to criminal court.

Demographics. In 2008, a majority of transfers involved youth who were at least age 17 in Florida (65%), Arizona (55%), and California (56%), but the racial and ethnic mix was quite different. In Florida, most transferred youth in 2008 were black (54%), whereas whites (29%) and Hispanics (12%) were considerably underrepresented. By contrast, transfers were predominantly Hispanic in Arizona (57%) and California (56%).

Offenses. In all three states, the vast majority of transfers involved felonies rather than misdemeanors. In 2008, 98% of reported transfers in Arizona, 89% in California, and 94% in Florida involved felonies, but transfer offenses in the three states differed substantially. In Florida, only 44% of reported 2008 transfers involved person offenses, whereas 31% involved property offenses and 11% involved drug offenses. Transfers were far more likely to involve person offenses in Arizona (60%) and California (65%).

Transfers for property offenses were less common in those states (25% in Arizona, 15% in California), as were transfers for drug offenses (6% in Arizona, 4% in California).

Case outcomes. As noted above, no comparison is possible among the three states with regard to the crucial issue of what happens to transferred youth—only California reports processing outcomes in transfer cases. However, because processing outcome information on transfer cases is so rare, it is worth noting that, over the period from 2003 through 2008, about three-quarters of cases involving juveniles disposed in California's criminal courts resulted in convictions. Following conviction, youth were sentenced to some form of incarceration (in a prison, jail, or California Youth Authority facility) in almost 8 of 10 cases.

Nearly 14,000 transfers can be accounted for in 2007—but most states are missing from that total

The size of the gaps in available transfer data can be broadly estimated

On the basis of juvenile court case processing data reported to the National Juvenile Court Data Archive, 8,500 judicial waivers are estimated to have occurred nationwide in 2007. The six states that track and report all of their nonjudicial transfers as well—Arizona, California, Florida, Michigan, Oregon, and Washington—reported an additional 5,096 nonjudicial transfer cases in 2007. Unpublished state-level information that Idaho provided to the Transfer Data Project contributed some 20 additional nonjudicial transfers to the 2007 total of 13,616.

A great deal is missing from this total, however—including nonjudicial transfers in the 29 other states that have statutory exclusion or prosecutorial discretion laws but do not publish statistics on criminal prosecution of juveniles and were not able to provide the Transfer Data Project with data from which 2007 totals could be derived. These 29 states fall into three basic groups.

States with extremely narrow nonjudicial transfer laws. In five of these states, transfer by means other than judicial waiver must be a very rare event. Massachusetts, Minnesota, and New Mexico have statutory exclusion provisions, but they apply only to juveniles accused of homicide. Utah has an exclusion law that, apart from homicide cases, covers only felonies that inmates in secure custody commit. Wisconsin's exclusion applies only to homicides and cases involving assaults committed against corrections, probation, and parole personnel. Even without knowing more, the authors can predict that the contribution to the nation's nonjudicial transfer total from these five states would be insignificant.

States with extremely broad nonjudicial transfer laws. At the other extreme, laws in two states—Nebraska and Vermont—authorize criminal prosecution of any 16- or 17-year-old youth, at the prosecutor's option, regardless of the offense alleged. In a third state—Wyoming—prosecutors have discretion to prosecute all misdemeanants in criminal court, as long as they are at least 13 years old. Laws of this exceptionally broad type are likely to generate large numbers of transfer cases, even though the states involved are not populous ones. In fact, criminal court data from Vermont, analyzed by NCJJ as part of a one-time study for that state's Agency for Human Services, found nearly 1,000 cases in which 16- and 17-year-old Vermont youth were handled as adults in a single year—a contribution to the nation's transfer total that would be comparable to California's published total in a typical year.

Other states. In the remaining 21 states, nonjudicial transfer provisions are much broader in scope than those in the first group but not so broad as those in the second. Youth are subject to nonjudicial transfer in these states for a range of offenses or offense types, all far more common than homicide. Nevertheless, they must meet some minimum threshold of offense seriousness. Some states within this middle group list specific offenses qualifying for nonjudicial transfer. In others, nonjudicial transfer laws do not merely apply to named offenses but also to felony offenses generally, or at least to felonies of a particular grade or grades.

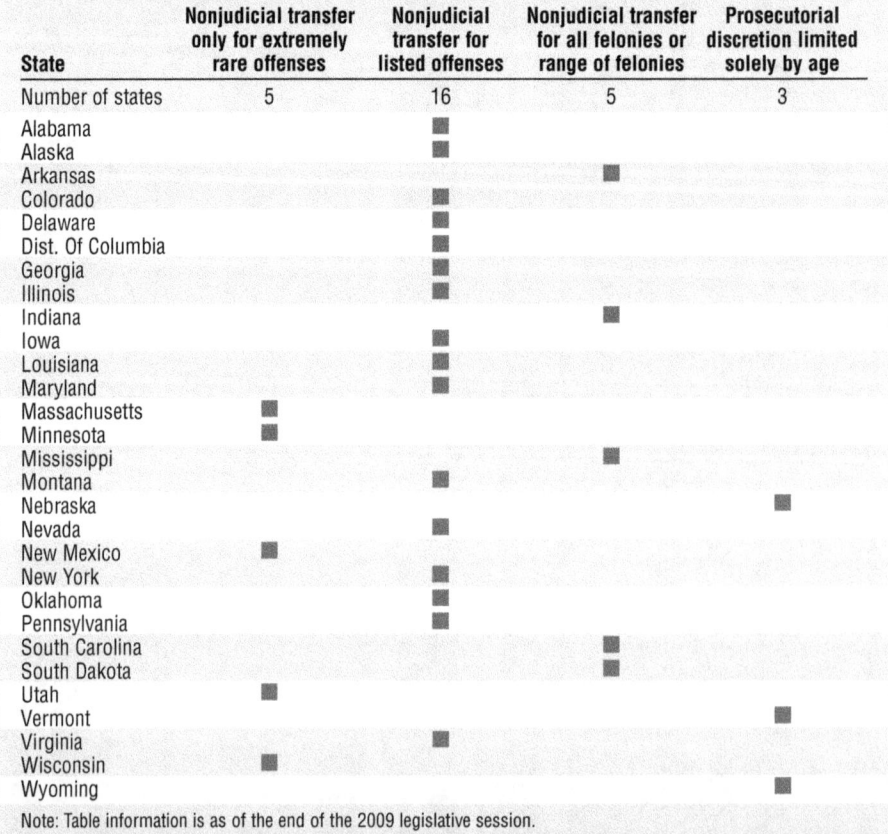

Among states that do not track and report nonjudicial transfers, the number unaccounted for depends on the scope of each state's laws

State	Nonjudicial transfer only for extremely rare offenses	Nonjudicial transfer for listed offenses	Nonjudicial transfer for all felonies or range of felonies	Prosecutorial discretion limited solely by age
Number of states	5	16	5	3
Alabama		■		
Alaska		■		
Arkansas			■	
Colorado		■		
Delaware		■		
Dist. Of Columbia		■		
Georgia		■		
Illinois		■		
Indiana			■	
Iowa		■		
Louisiana		■		
Maryland		■		
Massachusetts	■			
Minnesota	■			
Mississippi			■	
Montana		■		
Nebraska				■
Nevada		■		
New Mexico	■			
New York		■		
Oklahoma		■		
Pennsylvania		■		
South Carolina			■	
South Dakota			■	
Utah	■			
Vermont				■
Virginia		■		
Wisconsin	■			
Wyoming				■

Note: Table information is as of the end of the 2009 legislative session.

Jurisdictional age laws may "transfer" as many as 175,000 additional youth to criminal court

In 13 states, youth become criminally responsible before their 18th birthdays

Although it is important to have an idea of the number and characteristics of juveniles who are prosecuted as adults under state transfer laws, it should be remembered that most criminal prosecutions involving youth younger than 18 occur in states that limit the delinquency jurisdiction of their juvenile courts so as to exclude all 17-year-olds—or even all 16-year-olds—accused of crimes. States have always been free to define the respective jurisdictions of their juvenile and criminal courts. Nothing compels them to draw the line between "juvenile" and "adult" at the 18th birthday; in fact, there are 13 states that hold youth criminally responsible beginning with the 16th or

Upper age of original juvenile court jurisdiction, 2007

Age	State
15	Connecticut,* New York, North Carolina
16	Georgia, Illinois,** Louisiana, Massachusetts, Michigan, Missouri, New Hampshire, South Carolina, Texas, Wisconsin
17	Alabama, Alaska, Arizona, Arkansas, California, Colorado, Delaware, District of Columbia, Florida, Hawaii, Idaho, Indiana, Iowa, Kansas, Kentucky, Maine, Maryland, Minnesota, Mississippi, Montana, Nebraska, Nevada, New Jersey, New Mexico, North Dakota, Ohio, Oklahoma, Oregon, Pennsylvania, Rhode Island, South Dakota, Tennessee, Utah, Vermont, Virginia, Washington, West Virginia, Wyoming

* Upper age of original jurisdiction is being raised from 15 to 17: the transition will be complete by 2012.
** Upper age rose from 16 to 17 for those accused of misdemeanors only, effective 2010.

17th birthday. The number of youth younger than 18 prosecuted as adults in these states—not as exceptions, but as a matter of routine—can only be estimated. But it almost certainly dwarfs the number that reach criminal courts as a result of transfer laws in the nation as a whole.

A total of 2.2 million youth younger than 18 are subject to routine criminal processing

The authors do not know the number of youth prosecuted as adults in states that set the age of adult responsibility for crime at 16 or 17 for many of the same reasons that they do not know the number of youth prosecuted as adults under transfer laws. However, rough estimates are possible, based on population data and what is known about the offending behavior of 16- and 17-year-old youth.

In 2007, there were a total of 2.2 million 16- and 17-year-olds who were considered criminally responsible "adults" under the jurisdictional age laws of the states in which they resided. If one applies age-specific national delinquency case rates (the number of delinquency referrals per 1,000 juveniles) to this population group—and assume that they would have been referred to criminal court at the same rates that 16- and 17-year-olds are referred to juvenile courts in other states—then as many as 247,000 offenders younger than age 18 would have been referred to the criminal courts in 2007.

To determine the number of youth who are actually criminally prosecuted in the 13 states, delinquency case rates may be less pertinent than delinquency petition rates—that is, the age-specific rates at which youth are formally processed in (rather than merely referred to) juvenile

court. On the basis of age-specific delinquency petition rates, one would expect about 145,000 youth younger than 18 to have been criminally prosecuted in the 13 states in 2007.

It is possible to refine this rough estimate somewhat further. To account for the fact that different groups are formally processed in court at different rates, one can control not only for age but also for sex and race. If one applies age-, sex-, and race-specific petition rates to the population involved, an estimated 159,000 youth who were younger than 18 were prosecuted in criminal courts in the 13 states in 2007.

One can also take population density into account. The estimation procedure that NCJJ used to produce national data on juvenile court processing characteristics uses the county as the unit of aggregation. As part of the multiple-imputation and weighting process, all U.S. counties are placed into one of four strata on the basis of the size of their youth population, and specific rates are developed for age/race groups within each of the strata. If we apply similar age-, race-, and strata-specific petition rates to this population, we arrive at an estimate of 175,000 cases involving 16- or 17-year-olds tried in criminal court in the 13 states in 2007.

It should be noted again, however, that all of these estimates are based on an assumption that is at least questionable: that juvenile and criminal courts would respond in the same way to similar offending behavior. In fact, it is possible that some conduct that would be considered serious enough to merit referral to and formal processing in juvenile court—such as vandalism, trespassing, minor thefts, and low-level public order offenses—would not receive similar handling in criminal court.

Juveniles in most states can be jailed while awaiting trial in criminal court

Contact with adult inmates is sometimes but not always restricted

Depending on state law, local practice, and such factors as the age of the accused, juveniles who are confined while awaiting criminal trial may be held in juvenile detention facilities or adult jails.

A total of 48 states authorize jailing of juveniles who are awaiting trial in criminal court. In 14 of these states, use of adult jails rather than juvenile detention facilities for pretrial holding of transferred juveniles is mandated, at least in some circumstances; in the rest, the use of jails is allowed but not required. Sometimes a special court order or finding is required for jail holding, and sometimes a minimum age. For example, California requires a finding that a youth's pretrial detention in an ordinary juvenile facility would endanger the public or other juvenile detainees. In Illinois, a juvenile must be at least 15 to be held in jail, and a court must specifically order it. New Jersey requires a special hearing, comparable to a transfer hearing, before jail holding may be ordered. On the other hand, some states, such as Idaho and Tennessee, generally mandate use of jails for pretrial confinement when juveniles are processed as adults but empower courts to order the use of juvenile detention centers in individual cases.

Laws in 18 of the states that allow jail holding of juveniles specify that they must be kept from contact with adult jail inmates. Transferred youth in most states may also be held in juvenile detention facilities, either routinely or pursuant to court orders in individual cases.

Most states allow but do not require transferred youth to be held pretrial in adult jails rather than juvenile detention centers

State	Jailing of transferred youth allowed pending criminal trial	Minimum age, special condition, or court order required	Use of jails mandated under some circumstances	Youth–adult separation required
Number of states	48	15	14	18
Alabama	■		■	
Alaska	■			
Arizona	■			■
Arkansas	■			
California	■	■		■
Colorado	■	■		■
Connecticut	■		■	
Delaware	■	■	■	
District of Columbia	■			
Florida	■		■	■
Georgia	■	■		■
Hawaii	■		■	
Idaho	■		■	
Illinois	■	■		
Indiana	■			
Iowa	■	■		■
Kansas	■			■
Kentucky	■			■
Louisiana	■		■	
Maine	■	■		
Maryland	■		■	■
Massachusetts	■	■		
Michigan	■	■		
Minnesota	■			
Mississippi	■			
Missouri	■		■	
Montana	■			■
Nebraska	■	■		
Nevada	■			
New Hampshire	■		■	
New Jersey	■	■		
New Mexico	■		■	
New York	■	■		
North Carolina				
North Dakota	■			
Ohio	■			■
Oklahoma	■		■	
Oregon	■	■		
Pennsylvania	■			
Rhode Island	■			
South Carolina	■	■		
South Dakota	■			■
Tennessee	■		■	■
Texas	■			
Utah	■			■
Vermont	■	■		
Virginia	■			
Washington	■			
West Virginia			■	
Wisconsin	■		■	
Wyoming				

Note: New Mexico and Washington provisions apply only to previously convicted juveniles. Table information is as of the end of the 2009 legislative session.

A 2009 survey found that more than 7,000 youth who were younger than 18 were in jails

Federal data collections shed some light on state approaches to pretrial holding of transferred youth. The BJS-sponsored Annual Survey of Jails (ASJ) provides a one-day snapshot of the population confined in jails nationwide. According to the most recent ASJ, at midyear 2009 the nation's jails held a total of 7,220 inmates who were younger than 18, including 5,847 who had been tried or were awaiting trial as adults—less than 1% of the total jail population.

However, this cannot be considered an exact count of "transferred juveniles" in jail because many of these inmates who were younger than 18 were held in states where ordinary criminal court jurisdiction begins at age 16 or 17. Moreover, the total does not take account of inmates who were accused of offenses committed while younger than 18 but were already older than 18 by the time of the survey.

The Census of Juveniles in Residential Placement (CJRP) provides a one-day population count of the nation's juvenile facilities, including those normally used for detaining youth pending trial in the juvenile system. The most recent CJRP found that, as of the 2007 census date, a total of 1,101 individuals being held in juvenile residential facilities nationwide were awaiting proceedings in criminal court, in addition to 303 who were awaiting transfer hearings. Taken together, these youth made up about 1.6% of the residents of the nation's juvenile facilities.

Between 2005 and 2009, an average of 5,700 juveniles were held as adults in local jails—less than 1% of all inmates

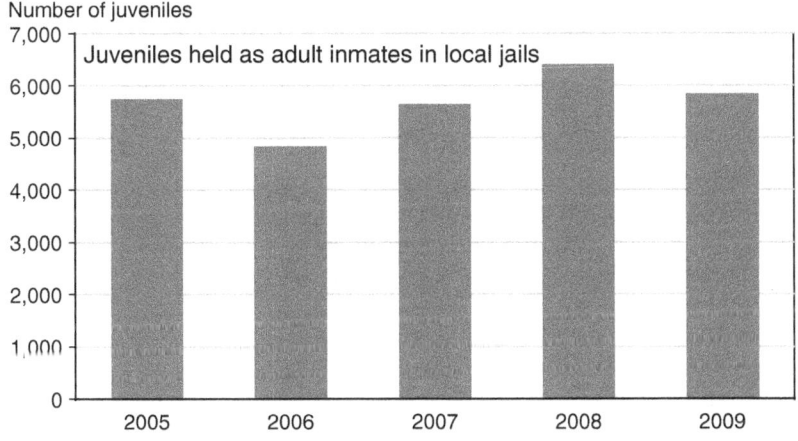

Number of juveniles

Juveniles held as adult inmates in local jails

Note: Authors' adaptation of Minton's Jail Inmates at Midyear 2009—Statistical Tables, *Prison and Jail Inmates at Midyear*.

Federal law prohibiting holding of juveniles with adults does not apply to transferred juveniles

The Juvenile Justice and Delinquency Prevention (JJDP) Act of 1974, as amended, generally requires, as a condition of federal funding for state juvenile justice systems, that juvenile delinquents and status offenders not be confined in jails or other facilities in which they have contact with incarcerated adults who have been convicted or are awaiting trial on criminal charges. However, regulations interpreting the JJDP Act provide that juveniles who are being tried as adults for felonies or have been criminally convicted of felonies may be held in adult facilities without violating this "sight and sound separation" mandate. Juveniles who have been transferred to the jurisdiction of a criminal court may also be confined with other juveniles in juvenile facilities without running afoul of the JJDP Act mandate. However, once these youth reach the state's maximum age of extended juvenile jurisdiction, they must be separated from the juvenile population.

The proposed Juvenile Justice and Delinquency Prevention Reauthorization Act of 2009, currently pending before Congress, would eliminate the special exception that permits jail holding of transferred juveniles while they await proceedings in criminal court. Effective 3 years from the enactment of the Reauthorization Act, the sight and sound separation mandate would apply to such youth. They could not be jailed with adults unless a court of competent jurisdiction, after considering a number of individualized factors, had determined that the interests of justice required it.

Convicted juveniles do not always receive harsher sanctions in the adult system

Sentencing and correctional handling of transferred youth vary from state to state

There are few national sources of information regarding what happens to youth once they are transferred to criminal courts. Even the most basic question—whether convicted youth are sanctioned more severely in the adult system than they would have been in the juvenile system—is difficult to answer, as various studies focusing on individual jurisdictions have yielded inconsistent results. On the one hand, most studies have concluded that criminal processing of these youth is more likely to result in incarceration and that periods of incarceration that criminal courts impose tend to be longer. However, a few have found no such differences in sentencing severity. In any case, it is likely that juvenile-criminal sentencing differences are largest in states that criminally prosecute only the most serious juvenile offenders. In states with transfer laws that apply to a broader range of less serious offenses, one would expect the adult system to regard transferred youth more lightly—and perhaps more lightly than the juvenile system would.

Special analyses of data from the State Court Processing Statistics Program (SCPS) and the National Judicial Reporting Program (NJRP) have shed some light on the ways in which criminal sentencing of transferred juvenile felons compares with dispositions of nontransferred youth on the one hand, and with sentencing of adult criminals on the other. In the first comparison, data on juvenile felony defendants from the 1990, 1992, and 1994 SCPS sample were contrasted with data on youth formally processed in the juvenile courts of the same large urban jurisdictions. Overall, 68% of the transferred

youth received sentences involving incarceration in jail or prison, whereas only 40% of the nontransferred youth received dispositions involving placement in juvenile correctional facilities. Of those convicted in criminal court of violent offenses, 79% were sentenced to incarceration, whereas only 44% of those adjudicated delinquent for violent offenses received juvenile dispositions involving placement. Similar criminal-juvenile differences were found in sanctions received by property offenders (57% incarcerated in the criminal system versus 35% in the juvenile system), drug offenders (50% versus 41%), and public order offenders (60% versus 46%).

A separate issue is whether, by reason of their age, juveniles in criminal court receive more lenient sentencing treatment than adult defendants. Analyses of 1996

NJRP data and 1998 SCPS data, comparing sentences that transferred juvenile felons received with sentences that adult felony defendants received, found no such consistent pattern of age-based leniency. Both studies found that transferred juveniles convicted of violent felonies were about as likely as adults to be sentenced to some form of incarceration. At least in the NJRP sample, juveniles convicted of property and weapons offenses were considerably more likely to be incarcerated than adult property and weapons offenders. Moreover, even though the NJRP analysis showed that transferred juveniles were sentenced to shorter maximum prison terms than were adults for sexual assault, burglary, and drug offense convictions, they received longer prison terms than adults did for murder and weapons offense convictions.

Among felony defendants convicted of property and weapons offenses, transferred juveniles were far more likely than adults to be sentenced to prison terms

Offense/ defendant	Profile of felony sentence imposed				Mean maximum sentence length (in months)		
	Total	Prison	Jail	Probation	Prison	Jail	Probation
All offenses							
Transferred juveniles	100%	60%	19%	21%	91	6	44
Adults	100	37	23	40	59	6	38
Violent offenses							
Transferred juveniles	100	75	9	15	118	8	55
Adults	100	78	5	17	101	7	46
Property offenses							
Transferred juveniles	100	46	27	27	39	6	43
Adults	100	18	28	54	46	6	38
Drug offenses							
Transferred juveniles	100	31	36	33	30	6	29
Adults	100	34	28	38	47	6	39
Weapons offenses							
Transferred juveniles	100	55	20	25	48	6	26
Adults	100	39	17	44	42	5	31
Other offenses							
Transferred juveniles	100	37	43	20	48	6	33
Adults	100	22	37	41	41	6	36

Source: Authors' adaptation of Levin, Langan, and Brown's *State Court Sentencing of Convicted Felons, 1996.*

Convicted youth may sometimes serve part of their sentences in juvenile facilities

States take a variety of correctional approaches with criminally convicted youth who receive sentences of incarceration, including straight incarceration in adult facilities with no distinction between minor and adult inmates, segregated incarceration in special facilities for underage offenders, and graduated incarceration that begins in juvenile facilities and is followed by later transfer to adult ones. According to juvenile correctional agencies responding to a 2008 survey that the Council of Juvenile Correctional Administrators conducted, in about two-thirds of states, juveniles who have been convicted and sentenced to incarceration by criminal courts may serve some portion of their sentences in juvenile correctional facilities.

Several states set a statutory minimum age—typically 16—for commitment to an adult correctional facility. In Delaware, for example, a youth younger than 16 who has been sentenced to a term of imprisonment must be held initially by the state's Division of Youth Rehabilitation Services and then transferred to the state's Department of Corrections upon reaching his or her 16th birthday.

The 2007 Census of Juveniles in Residential Placement counted a total of 761 inmates in juvenile residential facilities who had been convicted in criminal court and, presumably, were either serving their sentences or awaiting transfer to adult facilities.

State prisons, the bulk of them in the South, held more than 2,700 juveniles in 2009

At mid-year 2009, the National Prisoner Statistics Program, which collects one-day snapshot information on state prison inmates, counted a total of 2,778 inmates younger than age 18 in state prisons

nationwide. About 46% of these inmates were held in prisons in southern states.

Although many of these youth were undoubtedly convicted following prosecution under state transfer laws, more than half were held in states where ordinary criminal court jurisdiction begins at age 16 or 17 rather than 18.

Half of inmates younger than 18 held in state prisons come from states with a younger age of criminal responsibility

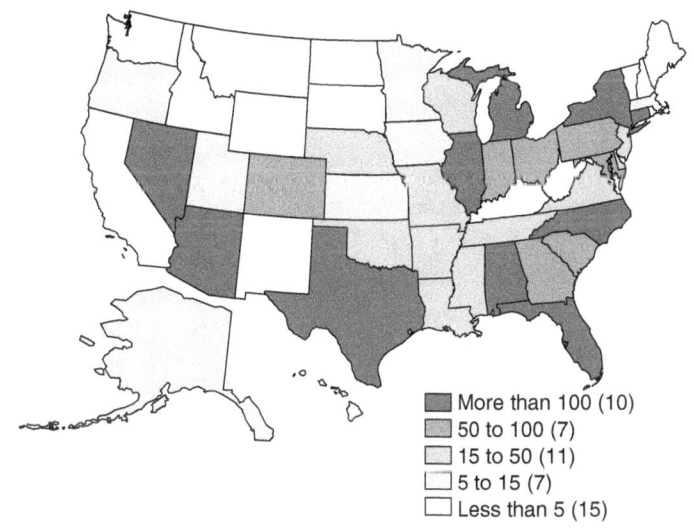

■ More than 100 (10)
■ 50 to 100 (7)
□ 15 to 50 (11)
□ 5 to 15 (7)
□ Less than 5 (15)

State	Inmates*	State	Inmates*	State	Inmates*
U.S. total	2,778	**Upper age 17**	**1,368**	Montana	1
		Alabama	118	Nebraska	21
Upper age 15	**737**	Alaska	7	Nevada	118
Connecticut	332	Arizona	157	New Jersey	21
New York	190	Arkansas	17	New Mexico	3
North Carolina	215	California	0	North Dakota	0
		Colorado	79	Ohio	86
Upper age 16	**673**	Delaware	28	Oklahoma	19
Georgia	99	Florida	393	Oregon	13
Illinois	106	Hawaii	2	Pennsylvania	61
Louisiana	15	Idaho	0	Rhode Island	1
Massachusetts	8	Indiana	54	South Dakota	1
Michigan	132	Iowa	13	Tennessee	22
Missouri	31	Kansas	5	Utah	6
New Hampshire	0	Kentucky	0	Vermont	4
South Carolina	89	Maine	0	Virginia	16
Texas	156	Maryland	58	Washington	2
Wisconsin	37	Minnesota	13	West Virginia	0
		Mississippi	28	Wyoming	1

* Reported number of inmates younger than age 18 held in custody in state prisons, 2009.

Source: Authors' adaptation of West's Prison Inmates at Midyear 2009—Statistical Tables, *Prison and Jail Inmates at Midyear*.

Transfer laws generally have not been shown to deter crime

Some research suggests that transfer may increase subsequent offending

Given the many practical ways in which state transfer laws vary in their scope and operation, blanket statements about their effects should be read with caution. However, insofar as these laws are intended to deter youth crime generally, or to deter or reduce further criminal behavior on the part of youth subjected to transfer, research over several decades has generally failed to establish their effectiveness.

Research on the general deterrence effects of transfer laws—their tendency to discourage the commission of offenses subject to transfer and criminal prosecution—has not produced entirely consistent results. Most studies have not found reductions in juvenile crime rates that can be linked to transfer laws. One multistate analysis by Levitt concluded that there could be a moderate general deterrent effect, and studies based on interviews with juveniles, conducted by Redding and Fuller and by Glassner and others, suggest the possibility that transfer laws could deter crime if sufficiently publicized. However, the weight of the evidence suggests that state transfer laws have little or no tendency to deter would-be juvenile criminals. Possible explanations include juveniles' general ignorance of transfer laws, tendency to discount or ignore risks in decisionmaking, and lack of impulse control.

A separate body of research, comparing postprocessing outcomes for criminally prosecuted youth with those of youth handled in the juvenile system, has uncovered what appear to be counter-deterrent effects of transfer laws. Six large-scale studies summarized by Redding—employing a range of different methodologies and measures of offending, and focusing on a variety of jurisdictions, populations, and types of transfer laws—have all found greater overall recidivism rates among juveniles who were prosecuted as adults than among matched youth who were retained in the juvenile system. Criminally prosecuted youth were also generally found to have recidivated sooner and more frequently. Poor outcomes like these could be attributable to a variety of causes, including the direct and indirect effects of criminal conviction on the life chances of transferred youth, the lack of access to rehabilitative resources in the adult corrections system, and the hazards of association with older criminal "mentors."

However, some critics have raised the possibility that the observed greater reoffending on the part of transferred youth is simply a consequence of group differences between transferred and nontransferred youth—not an effect of transfer but a "selection bias" that could not be corrected for, given the limited information and statistical controls available to researchers. (See, for example, Meyers' study "The Recidivism of Violent Youths in Juvenile and Adult Court: A Consideration of Selection Bias.")

The studies finding that transfer had counterdeterrent effects did not all agree in finding these effects for all offense types—leaving open the possibility that criminal prosecution may work for some kinds of young offenders and not work for others. In fact, a 2010 comparison, by Schubert and others, of rearrest outcomes for transferred and nontransferred youth found that, whereas transfer appeared to have no effect on rearrest rates for the sample as a whole, transferred person offenders had lower rearrest rates than their nontransferred counterparts.

Although transfer laws in general have not been shown to work (that is, improve public safety by reducing serious crime through specific or general deterrence), it is not clear whether this conclusion applies to all transfer laws equally because the key studies have been conducted in only a handful of states. Again, it should be remembered that transfer laws vary considerably, and their effects are unlikely to be uniform. It may be that some transfer provisions—targeting certain offenses or resulting in certain sanctions—are more effective in deterring crime than others.

The data gathered under BJS's new Survey of Juveniles Charged in Adult Criminal Courts should significantly contribute to our understanding of the national impact of state transfer mechanisms but is unlikely to support state-level analyses. Better state-level data are necessary to support the state-specific research that is clearly needed to shed light on the impact and workings of each state's transfer laws.

Sources

Adams, B., and Addie, S. 2010. Delinquency Cases Waived to Criminal Court, 2007. *OJJDP Fact Sheet*. Washington, DC: U.S. Department of Justice, Office of Justice Programs, Office of Juvenile Justice and Delinquency Prevention.

Federal Bureau of Investigation. Unpublished arrest statistics reports for 1980 through 1997.

Federal Bureau of Investigation. Various. *Crime in the United States* for the years 1998 through 2003. Washington, DC: U.S. Government Printing Office.

Federal Bureau of Investigation. *Crime in the United States* for the years 2004 through 2008. Available online at www.fbi.gov/ucr/ucr.htm#cius, released September 2009.

Feld, B. 1987. The Juvenile Court Meets the Principle of the Offense: Legislative Changes to Juvenile Waiver Statutes. *Journal of Criminal Law and Criminology* 78(3):471–533.

Glassner, B., Ksander, M., Berg, B., and Johnson, B.D. 1983. A Note on the Deterrent Effect of Juvenile Versus Adult Jurisdiction. *Social Problems* 31:219–21.

Griffin, P., Thomas, D., and Puzzanchera, C. 2007. *Final Report: Juvenile Justice Jurisdiction Study*. Submitted to Vermont Agency of Human Services Juvenile Justice Commission, Children and Family Council for Prevention Programs. Pittsburgh, PA: National Center for Juvenile Justice.

Hutzler, J. 1980. *Juveniles as Criminals: 1980 Statutes Analysis*. Pittsburgh, PA: National Center for Juvenile Justice.

Levin, D., Langan, P., and Brown, J. 2000. *State Court Sentencing of Convicted Felons, 1996*. Washington, DC: U.S. Department of Justice, Office of Justice Programs, Bureau of Justice Statistics.

Levitt, S.D. 1998. Juvenile Crime and Punishment. *Journal of Political Economy* 106:1156–85.

Loughran, E.J., Godfrey, K., Dugan, B., and Mengers, L. 2009. *CJCA Yearbook 2009: A National Perspective of Juvenile Corrections*. Braintree, MA: Council of Juvenile Correctional Administrators.

Meyers, D.L. 2003. The Recidivism of Violent Youths in Juvenile and Adult Court: A Consideration of Selection Bias. *Youth Violence and Juvenile Justice* 1:79–101.

Minton, T. 2010. Jail Inmates at Midyear 2009—Statistical Tables. *Prison and Jail Inmates at Midyear*. Washington, DC: U.S. Department of Justice, Office of Justice Programs, Bureau of Justice Statistics.

Perry, S. 2006. *Prosecutors in State Courts, 2005*. Washington, DC: U.S. Department of Justice, Office of Justice Programs, Bureau of Justice Statistics.

Puzzanchera, C., Adams, B., and Sickmund, M. 2010. *Juvenile Court Statistics 2007*. Pittsburgh, PA: National Center for Juvenile Justice.

Rainville, G., and Smith, S. 2003. *Juvenile Felony Defendants in Criminal Courts: Survey of 40 Counties, 1998*. Washington, DC: U.S. Department of Justice, Office of Justice Programs, Bureau of Justice Statistics.

Redding, R. 2010. Juvenile Transfer Laws: An Effective Deterrent to Delinquency? *OJJDP Bulletin*. Washington, DC: U.S. Department of Justice, Office of Justice Programs, Office of Juvenile Justice and Delinquency Prevention.

Redding, R.E., and Fuller, E.J. 2004 (Summer). What Do Juvenile Offenders Know About Being Tried as Adults? Implications for Deterrence. *Juvenile and Family Court Journal* 35–45.

Sabol, W., and West, H. 2009. Prison Inmates at Midyear 2008—Statistical Tables. *Prison and Jail Inmates at Midyear*. Washington, DC: U.S. Department of Justice, Office of Justice Programs, Bureau of Justice Statistics.

Schubert, C., Mulvey, E., Loughran, T., Fagan, J., and Chassin, L., et al. 2010. Predicting Outcomes for Youth Transferred to Adult Court. *Law and Human Behavior* 34(6):460–75.

Schubert, C., Mulvey, E., Loughran, T., Chassin, L., and Steinberg, L., et al. Differential Effects of Adult Court Transfer on Juvenile Offender Recidivism. *Law and Human Behavior* 34(6):476–88.

Sickmund, M., Sladky, A., and Kang, W. 2010. *Easy Access to Juvenile Court Statistics: 1985–2007* [online analysis]. Available at ojjdp.gov/ojstatbb/ezajcs.

Sickmund, M., Sladky, T.J., Kang, W., and Puzzanchera, C. Forthcoming. *Easy Access to the Census of Juveniles in Residential Placement: 1997–2007* [online analysis]. Available at www.ojjdp.gov/ojstatbb/ezacjrp.

Strom, K., Smith, S., and Snyder, H. 1998. *Juvenile Felony Defendants in Criminal Courts: State Court Processing Statistics, 1990–94*. Washington, DC: U.S. Department of Justice, Office of Justice Programs, Bureau of Justice Statistics.

Torbet, P., Gable, R., Hurst, H., Montgomery, I., Szymanski, L., and Thomas, D. 1996. *State Responses to Serious and Violent Juvenile Crime*. Washington, DC: U.S. Department of Justice, Office of Justice Programs, Office of Juvenile Justice and Delinquency Prevention.

Torbet, P., and Szymanski, L. 1998. *State Legislative Responses to Violent Juvenile Crime: 1996–97 Update*. Washington, DC: U.S. Department of Justice, Office of Justice Programs, Office of Juvenile Justice and Delinquency Prevention.

West, H. 2010. Prison Inmates at Midyear 2009—Statistical Tables. *Prison and Jail Inmates at Midyear*. Washington, DC: U.S. Department of Justice, Office of Justice Programs, Bureau of Justice Statistics.

The authors used the following state reports:

Arizona Administrative Office of the Courts. Available at http://www.azcourts.gov/jjsd/PublicationsReports.aspx.

California Office of the Attorney General. Available at http://ag.ca.gov/crime.php.

Florida Office of the State Courts Administrator. Available at http://www.flcourts.org/gen_public/stats.

Kansas Judicial Branch. Available at http://judicial.kscourts.org:7780/stats.

Michigan State Court Administrative Office. Available at http://courts.michigan.gov/scao/resources/publications.

Missouri Department of Social Services. Available at http://www.dss.mo.gov/re/jcsar.htm.

Montana Board of Crime Control. Available at http://www.mbcc.mt.gov/JuvenileJustice/JuvJustice.asp.

North Carolina Department of Juvenile Justice and Delinquency Prevention. Available at http://www.juvjus.state.nc.us/statistics/statistics.html.

Supreme Court of Ohio. Available at http://www.sconet.state.oh.us/publications.

Oregon Youth Authority. Available at http://www.oregon.gov/OYA/jjis_data_eval_rpts.shtml.

Tennessee Council of Juvenile and Family Court Judges. Available at http://www.tn.gov/tcjfcj/annualrpt.html.

Texas Office of Court Administration. Available at http://www.courts.state.tx.us/pubs/pubs-home.asp.

Washington State Sentencing Guidelines Commission. Available at http://www.sgc.wa.gov/Informational/Publications.htm.

Acknowledgments

This Bulletin was written by Patrick Griffin, Senior Research Associate, Sean Addie, Policy Analyst, Benjamin Adams, Research Associate, and Kathy Firestine, Research Assistant, at the National Center for Juvenile Justice, with funds provided by OJJDP to support the National Juvenile Justice Data Analysis Project.

This Bulletin was prepared under cooperative agreement number 2008–JF–FX–K071 from the Office of Juvenile Justice and Delinquency Prevention (OJJDP), U.S. Department of Justice.

Points of view or opinions expressed in this document are those of the authors and do not necessarily represent the official position or policies of OJJDP or the U.S. Department of Justice.

The Office of Juvenile Justice and Delinquency Prevention is a component of the Office of Justice Programs, which also includes the Bureau of Justice Assistance; the Bureau of Justice Statistics; the National Institute of Justice; the Office for Victims of Crime; and the Office of Sex Offender Sentencing, Monitoring, Apprehending, Registering, and Tracking.